W9-APM-692

Rookie
Read-About®
Holidays

Valentine's Day

by Trudi Strain Trueit

Content Consultants

Nanci R. Vargus, Ed.D.
Professor Emeritus, University of Indianapolis

Carrie A. Bell, MST — All Grades
Julia A. Stark Elementary School, Stamford, Connecticut

Reading Consultant

Jeanne M. Clidas, Ph.D.
Reading Specialist

Children's Press®
An Imprint of Scholastic Inc.
New York Toronto London Auckland Sydney
Mexico City New Delhi Hong Kong
Danbury, Connecticut

Library of Congress Cataloging-in-Publication Data
Trueit, Trudi Strain.
  Valentine's day / by Trudi Strain Trueit.
    pages cm. — (Rookie read-about holidays)
  Includes index.
  ISBN 978-0-531-27207-7 (library binding) — ISBN 978-0-531-27357-9 (pbk.)
  1. Valentine's Day—Juvenile literature. I. Title.
  GT4925.T78 2013
  394.2618—dc23   2013014850

Produced by Spooky Cheetah Press

Printed in China 62

1 2 3 4 5 6 7 8 9 10 R 23 22 21 20 19 18 17 16 15 14

Photographs © 2014: Adam Chinitz: 28; AP Images: 4 (Andrew Poertner/Roswell Daily
Record), 15, 31 center bottom (North Wind Picture Archives); Getty Images/Boston
Globe: 22; iStockphoto/Rosemarie Gearhart/Artistic Captures: 10; Louise Gardner:
7; Media Bakery: 9 (Armadillo Stock), 16, 31 center top (Circa), cover (Daniel Grill),
24 (Rob Lewine/Tetra Images); PhotoEdit/Michael Newman: 18, 27, 30 left, 31 top;
Shutterstock, Inc./Elena Gaak: 3 bottom; Superstock, Inc./Cusp: 30 right; The Image
Works: 12 (akg-images), 21, 31 bottom (SJkold); Thinkstock/Comstock: 3 top.

Table of Contents

These kids made valentine crowns and cards for a class party.

4

Saying "I Love You!"

What a wonderful surprise—a pretty **valentine** from a good friend! Today is a very special day.

Valentine's Day is February 14th. Millions of people in the United States **celebrate** the holiday. People in many other countries celebrate Valentine's Day, too.

Valentine's Day is celebrated on the same date every year.

FEBRUARY

SUNDAY	MONDAY	TUESDAY	WEDNESDAY	THURSDAY	FRIDAY	SATURDAY
						1
2	3	4	5	6	7	8
9	10	11	12	13	14	15
16	17	18	19	20	21	22
23	24	25	26	27	28	

7

This is a day to tell people you care about them. You could give a valentine to your teacher. Some people even give Valentine's Day gifts to their pets!

FAST FACT!

Do you know who gets the most cards and gifts on Valentine's Day? Teachers!

Valentine's Day is about love and friendship. Whom do you love? Your mom and dad? How about your best friend?

Valentine's Day is a great time to tell our friends how much we care.

IMP · C · M · AVR · CLAVDIVS · P · F · AVG · GERM · GOTTHICVS

12

How It Began

A long time ago, a priest named Valentine lived in Rome. The ruler of Rome made it against the law for people to get married.

This picture shows the Roman ruler on an ancient coin.

13

Valentine helped people get married in secret. He was put in jail for this. Then, the Roman ruler had him killed on February 14th.

To honor him, the priests made that day **Saint** Valentine's Day.

Valentine helped people get married without anyone knowing.

14

15

TRUE

LOVE

This bow of Red,
Is Cupid's choice,
I send it to you
For better or worse;
Oh will't be mine,
My Valentine.

TO MY
VALENTINE

Years later, a man in a French jail wrote **poetry** to his wife. When people heard this story, they called the man's poems "valentines." That started the tradition of sending poems and notes to people on Valentine's Day.

Some early Valentine's Day cards were decorated with lace and even gold!

Be My Valentine

Today we celebrate Valentine's Day in many different ways. Sometimes we have parties in school.

This girl is putting valentines for her classmates in a homemade mailbox.

Some people make their own cards. Others buy them. Some people sign their name to the cards. Others do not!

FAST FACT!

Every Valentine's Day, people around the world give out one billion valentines! That makes Valentine's Day the second-largest holiday for giving greeting cards.

Some children visit people in hospitals or senior centers on Valentine's Day. This is a great way to make someone feel special.

People may also give gifts on Valentine's Day. They may give someone flowers or balloons.

This boy is giving his mother flowers for Valentine's Day.

Some people give chocolate or candy hearts to the people they care about. How will *you* celebrate Valentine's Day?

These friends are sharing a Valentine's Day treat.

Make a Valentine's Day Card

What You'll Need

- Red and white construction paper
  (For a simpler card, substitute a red
  heart doily for the red construction paper.
  See below.)
- Pencil

- Scissors
- Glue stick
- Crayons or markers
- Glitter

Directions

1. With an adult's help, fold the red paper in half and use a pencil to draw half a heart on the fold. Cut it out. Repeat with the white paper, but make this heart smaller than the first. Open the cutouts to discover two hearts.

2. Glue the white heart on top of the red heart.

3. Using crayons or markers, decorate your card with words, hearts, curly lines, or any designs you wish!

4. Use the glue to add glitter wherever you'd like. Make the design with the glue stick, sprinkle glitter onto the valentine over a trash can, and shake off extra glitter.

For a simpler valentine, cut a small square out of the white paper and glue it to the center of the heart doily. Write a Valentine's Day message on the square. Add any other decorations you'd like.

Show What You Know!

A Very Special Day

Traditions are things that people do year after year. They make a holiday special.

- Which of these photos shows a Valentine's Day tradition? Why?
- Does your family have Valentine's Day traditions? What are they?
- Ask your parents or teacher to share traditions from when they were young.

A Valentine's Day to Remember

- Ask a parent or guardian to share his or her happiest Valentine's Day memory with you. What made it so special?
- What is your favorite Valentine's Day memory?

Glossary

celebrate (SEH-luh-brayt): to do something fun on a special occasion

poetry (POH-uh-tree): written verses that may or may not rhyme

saint (SAYNT): a person honored by the Christian church because of his or her holy life

valentine (VA-luhn-tine): a gift or card sent on Valentine's Day; a loved one chosen on Valentine's Day

Index

Facts for Now

Visit this Scholastic Web site for more information on Valentine's Day:
www.factsfornow.scholastic.com
Enter the keywords **Valentine's Day**

About the Author

Trudi Strain Trueit has written more than 80 fiction and nonfiction books for children. She is also the author of *Christmas* in the Rookie Read-About Holidays series. She was born and raised and still lives in the Pacific Northwest. Valentine's Day is her favorite holiday because she gets to spend it with her valentine, Bill, and her favorite food, chocolate!